NAKED HUMAN
WRITTEN AND ARRANGED BY CHRISTOPHER POINDEXTER
FEATURING WORK BY ANTHONY GREEN

cover art by Jason Markow [tekstartist]
http://fivespotderby.com
back cover and interior artwork by Zach Landrum
www.oldesoulprintshop.com
additional art by Valerie Kalinin & MaryAnn Santana

WRITTEN BETWEEN 2012-2015 IN
NEW ORLEANS, LA / CAMDEN, AR / MANHATTAN, NY
LOS ANGELES, CA / LONG BEACH, CA / DALLAS, TX

this book is dedicated to many things and people. It is a tiny collection of my thoughts and experiences over the past three years and my aim was to attempt to understand things that most people don't try to. this is for the human race as a whole. we are such magical creatures. This is for my lovely woman Lei Rebadomia. I love you more than life baby. Also for my mother, the sweetest thing on planet earth. For my father, a mad man on the outside, but deep down one of the most sincere spirits I know. This is for you, the one reading this, may we never forget we are all in this together.

CONTENTS

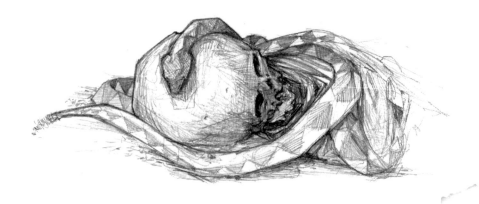

NAKED HUMAN

BY

CHRISTOPHER POINDEXTER

YOU ARE ETHEREAL

i will shed
all of this skin
down to the
very bone beneath
it
if that's what
it will take
for you
to come to the
realization
that appearance
is not what makes
a human
beautiful.

you're as sweet as anything
is sweet

as warm as anything
is warm

i connect our days together
like constellations
mapping out numbers
that will allow us
to light up
the entire earth

and as my mind beats
with the thrilling
thought of you
rolling over
in sheets of
infinity

i am certain
the equation
equals forever

"i am something new"
you must tell yourself.
"i am the beginning and
end
of a story that will
never be lived again.
i am new earth and
new air and
new words.
i am as fresh as
birth.
i am significant."

every morning i see a cup of coffee
in front of my sleepy eyes but i am
starting to see things differently,
because of you.
now i see beans, once tossed in hands
and broken down in machines
and placed in bags
sent off somewhere
where the tired people gather.
i see that only because your tenderness
has taught me that we must look beyond
the body of everything and into the soul of all.

how heartbreaking
it is
that people are
so quick
to tilt their
clumsy chins
downward to
others
who do not
want the same things
as them.
why the hell
must we,
all vessels
of the human race,
keep looking
away when we
see a face
we do
not understand?

nestle up with me now and let us
fall in love with the feeling
of our worries spilling into the sheets.
nestle up with me now,
let us give birth to seeds of whispering moans
and let those coil with our bones
as we tumble in love with the blooming echo.
nestle up with me now,
let us grow old and die delicate in each other's arms,
for my god what an exquisite honor it would be
to erode from this crumbling earth
all the while being washed in your
lover's grains.

nestle up with me.

it was you and i that night
by the sea,
two bottles of wine and
a bowl deep,
we kissed and made love
as the moon and waves
talked business.

waking up
bare feet hitting
the crystal floor
i have two options
as i always do-
i can focus on all
that i am,
human and blossoming into
something necessary
and luminous,
or
i can focus on all
that i am not
which the list goes
on and on
things i wish i were.

it is all up to me.
the choice is always mine.

i, am treasure.

i'll throw
my
voice into
the stars and maybe
the echo of my words will
be written for you
in the clouds by
sunrise.
all i am trying
to say is,
I will love you
through the darkness.

legends are built from
souls like hers.
the kind that no one
ever really hears about
until they see the
monuments.

"I am yours my dear"
i whispered.

"i would rather fall in love
with the tragically ignored
than the easily accepted."

I get lost in other
people's lives.
finding beauty in theirs
has always been easier
than finding it in my own.
sometimes i feel as if I
am made up entirely of
human beings-
the pain I see in their
quiet eyes,
the joy that glistens from
their skin when something
makes them happy.

this is enough for me.
it always has been.

i will take this beauty
to my grave.

there is an alcoholic in
my neighborhood no one
ever talks to.
the neighbors don't wave or stare,
he is just there sipping away
12 pack after 12 pack
pint after pint
day after day after day.
it is like everyone already considers his
mind gone. his human hands no good
for doing good.
one morning my lady turned to me as
we were watching him get his morning
paper off the lawn and said, "baby, let's
bring him a few bottles.
the best scotch we can find."

so we did. and he welcomed
us with a smile. my goodness, were
his stories endless. and perfect.

i must say, i loved her for that. for simple refusing
to do what everyone else does.

spontaneous kindness
may be this planet's only hope.

the details of anything you love are
always what is most thrilling, most poignant,
most important.
i loved her as she rose from bed and fell back
against it again, and all she did in-between.
when you love someone you accept them,
you become them in a way, and all they
do forms into you. their mannerisms turn
into truth- the way she holds her favorite coffee mug,
the way she laughs, the way she smells, the way her lips
curl after certain words. all of the simple things
suddenly become gigantic things and light up the world
before you like a flame thrown into the clouds.
what a breathtaking display. the way
the earth begins to dissolve in your periphery
and a human being replaces it.

no matter what they tell you-
a person is a universe when truly
loved and anything less is not
love at all.

the world only remembers what
you did moments ago.
you are defined by the burning
seconds before you.
so i say cheers to this-
be relentless with your passion.
with your art. with your love.
not for the sake of others,
but for yourself. for your
golden voice.
create wonderful things
as if only those things
spin the hands of time
itself.

it is the feeling of never knowing
what we want that truly drives us
all mad. what is more terrible
than that?
holding things because
we think in a moment
we love them only to uncurl
our fingers later and softly
give them back
to the earth.

i have this dream where i keep
all of my favorite feelings
in mason jars
and bring them out
and open them when
i feel empty

i call the
dream 'paradise'

not because all
of the feelings
are happy

but because i
am in love
with feeling a
little bit of everything.

all we
ever really
want
is for something
extraordinary
to happen.
something that
doesn't fit the
routine
of sunrise,
sunset,
sleep
and dream.
there are
those who wait
for it,
their hands steady below
their waist
and
there are those
who create it,
their arms
like a spiral
staircase
to the stars.

ask yourself,
which
one are you?

THE PRINCE WE CALL BALANCE

tell me i am fucking crazy
for turning so quickly
from a happy man to a
broken man.
what they don't understand
and cannot seem to get
through their thick skulls
is that to reach the broken
people, you too, have to
be broken. and that,
is all i have ever wanted-
to reach people,
people no one has yet
reached.

so i will say this-
give me your suffering
and i swear it will be carried
even if that means the death
of sorrow inside you
and the birth of sorrow
inside me.

some days i am just completely empty
and to be honest those are the days
i drink the most. what do i drink for?
to be filled, of course. why does anyone
who feels nothing do whatever it is
they do to feel something?

my father used to sit on our porch
with a cigarette in one hand and a
beer in the other and just drink and smoke
until the world felt different
and it took me years to understand
that wasn't a terrible thing,
but rather, a beautiful reflection
of the human spirit.

the thing about
chaos,
is that while
it disturbs us,
it too
forces our hearts
to roar in a way
we secretly
find magnificent.

the best thing we can do is be honest
about our souls.
i have learned about myself that at times
i am filled with an incredible
amount of warm sadness
because there are just too many
extraordinary people in this world
for me.
i feel like i could love
a thousand different people and live
a thousand different lives
in just this one body
i have been given.
that is why i am such a dangerous lover-
you do not want to fall in love with me.
i will burn your world down ferociously.
i run with packs of wolves
and my blood stricken fangs
have fallen in love with the tragedy
that i yearn to fall in love
with you. and you and you and

you.

give me the world
but for Christ's sake,
do not sugarcoat it.
give me it raw
and gleaming with
truth.
i want the madness
to twirl me around until
i can no longer stand.
i refuse to be drunk
on a soft world.
the world is cruel,
my love,
you must understand
that,
but in that understanding
you must understand this,
too, just because it is cruel
does not mean it is not
beautiful.

every day i walk my dogs around the
block and pass this house where a
young man i hardly knew overdosed
only years ago.
i remember seeing his
red truck drive by every day,
him smoking a cigarette,
routine wave.
the truck just sits there now,
the morning sun beaming off of it loudly
as if the universe is trying to
tell me something.
"don't be like him."
i hear in a ruffled murmur.
"he was beautiful, and his spirit
still lives in the air. think of him
not less than anyone else."
i hear more clearly.

i must never stop finding the humanness
in people like him. so, every day
i pass by his home i never forget to
kiss the tips of my fingers and send
it towards that bright red automobile,
picturing in me head that he is
driving it, smoking a cigarette,
and being nothing but human.

drowning myself intimately in booze
every day for the past two years, it has
been a wild ride. i began to drink to discover
some kind of ill code that lived inside
my drunken father, a code i never understood
as a child. now i sit here numb in this bath filled
up to my chest, knees into it, pacing myself back
and forth back and forth. i live with this
growing belly now, it is like a scar, a punishment
for being weak, for not being able to feel
anything without heaping myself
into the bottom of a bottle. who knew when you
were standing in front of churches, christopher,
preaching to the bodies in the pews, that it all
would come to this. who ever knows where our
ill minds go to and why they go to wherever
they go. we just let them i suppose. but i do remember
the root of it all. i used to tell myself
"i drink to understand those i do not know.
to feel what they feel. what he feels. what she feels."
it is similar to my favorite bible verse but played with
a little "to the drunkard i become the drunkard. to the
stoner i become the stoner. to the weeping man i
become the weeping man."

a young gay man sits on a balcony fifty stories
up, cigarette in his mouth, drink in his hand.
he stares out into the waves, into oblivion.
the air is cold and unsure. quick as a cat
and soft as freedom. he thinks of the
world against him-
the jokers and the judgers, the politicians
and the churches.
he closes his eyes and breathes into himself-
"i am what i am supposed to be.
i am fucking free."
he opens them and the moon has turned the
color red.
he smiles and goes to bed
knowing the universe loves him
even when the world
is too stupid to do
so.

they cursed him
an alcoholic
ruined by
the misery of
losing the only
woman he ever purely
loved.
they judged him
gave him a figure
of a dancer
no longer able
to dance.
they forgot his pain,
remembered their
close-mindedness,
carried it with them
always
everywhere they went.

in the heart of a drunkard
they saw nothing, absolutely
nothing,

what a fucking shame.

being an asshole is
a business

i can see them now-
gathered around a
cherry wood table
with blueprints
that lead to innocent people's
tears.

i am so exhausted dealing with them
as i go get my morning coffee
and midnight wine
but the truth of the truth is,
a truth i so often
am afraid to admit,
they, more so than us
(the ones who choose to quarrel
over their faults)
need love too.

we must fight hate with sweetness.

sometimes
i just feel impossible.
like life wasn't meant
for me.
like it was an
interview
i showed up too
drunk out of
my mind.

i think we are and will always
be lonely people in a lonely
world under lonely stars.
we can never starve our loneliness.
we can only hope that by the
company of others,
is doesn't devour us.

she was the kind of woman
who only gave herself away in small doses,
leaving men wondering like little children
at all that she was.
she tortured them with the sound
of her fading footsteps,
each one an exclamation mark
to a sentence the world tragically
instilled in her long ago
"find something beautiful, then
let it go."

the problem is you think
you are not magic.
from any distance you
appear as all things stunning
do- they force us to forfeit
all we knew before.
you are exploding stars
and fearfully forgotten truths,
the way the ocean sways
and ever so illuminating
moons.
you are as magic as magic
gets,
as brilliant as brilliance is,
as unexplainably beautiful
as anything has ever been.
to think you are not magic,
well, darling,
i suppose even our thoughts
can betray us and be
fools.

i truly believe if we love
enough
the earth will love us back.
you are made of wind
and fire
and rain
and dust
and as long as you spread kindness
consistently and abundantly,
the flowers and trees
will grant you freedom.

your body will be so warm,
the sun will ask you to dance,
and you will feel so wonderful,
there is no way you
wouldn't say
yes.

i still have
the scarlet scarf
you gave me.
it smells of your
wild freedom.

if only we
could
feel what
we remember
and not just
remember
what we
felt.

- a note from mother universe

when a human treats you badly my son, close your eyes,
breathe deeply, and feel me tall in your chest. that is not
only the sky and ocean, that is a whole human race inside you.
never forfeit what you believe- all of you began naked. keep
being ridiculous while people tell you to give up hope
in the cruel. give so much love, it haunts the hate in others.
they will think your gift is silly, that you are just another
wannabe modern day hippie, but show them that there
is so much more to this. to you. to them. keep
being ridiculous in the most purest of ways.
not enough people are.

DELICACY

I have always thought, and I may be
the only one, that the famous saying
"you must love yourself before you
can love anyone else," was complete
bullshit. especially for those of us
who were not born with perfect bodies
or bone structures or a gift to find
the right words. I believe for us,
that only by falling hopelessly in love
and being hopelessly loved back, do we
begin to learn to love all that we are
and truthfully, the person we have
always been.

i have so many things
inside me
i loathe.
i learned when i was young
the way to live
is to give yourself away
to people who need you, who need
love,
but a decade later and
i still marry my flesh
each morning.
"i give myself to you, boy.
fuck the others"
the flesh says to me,

my heart weeping
quietly for deliverance
somewhere in a
corner.

the gate around
heaven was
crowded when we
arrived together.
you looked at me
and giggled
and with whiskey on
your rose breath
you led me to some
place higher.

i always knew you were
beyond them.
i just wasn't sure
how far.

so let me
get this straight,
down to the marrow of the bone,
to the monstrous unsavory
truth-
we breathe air
in a world
where
the people are more
obsessed with gorgeous
bodies that one day
rot away,
than gorgeous souls
that weep
handsomely
like violins
into infinity?

my god, little precious creatures,
we, yes we, you and i and he and she,
have so many things
wrong.

a sweet woman
like you
can truly
make
a wild man
like me
want to settle
down

your ass
was
a gateway
drug
to your soul

I could be like the rest of them,
and say a piece of me dies
when you leave my touch.
I have said it before.
but the truth? I never die.
i am simply reborn in
your distance.

I am a version of my
solitude
that knows I have you.
There is no reason to ache.

being alone fuels our
flame even more.

when the wine is gone
and you remove your tired body from
your steaming bath, come to bed.
do not worry about putting
on your night clothes, naked you'll
come as you know the moon
loves the sight of your bare flesh
through the window.
the sheets are calling your name
my dear.
come as you are.
there is enough love
in me to birth an entirely
new universe and to it
we can run whenever this world
becomes too heavy for our
shaking shoulders.

throw everything
i've ever wanted
away
and send it somewhere
I will never find it
and don't ever
bring it back
until i find
what it means to
make someone
else's life
my own

if darkness is
really not
darkness
at all,
but rather,
the absence of
light,
then my flaws
are not really
flaws at all,
but rather,
the absence of
you.

they ask you
how does it feel
to be so small,
standing knightly
in their elegant
castles
looking down on you
with such impure
disgust.
if i have ever told
you anything meaningful,
let it be this-

fuck that.
fuck their words.
be who you are,
even if it hurts.

atheists
are flowers
torn apart
by the minds
of the
religious.

i've built a
radio
from the world's
weeping.
each morning i
must sit down at my desk,
sip some champagne,
smoke a few cigarettes,
and with ears that soak
in noise
like a mother
soaking
in her child's
laughter,
i must listen.
to the cries.
to the stories.
to the tragedy.
to the pain.

oddly,
this little nook has
become my favorite
place.

an older man once said to me
on a park bench after i spilled my
sensitivity out to him
"you better be able
to take a punch from the ones
more beautiful than you, kid.
or else you will never make it."

but this is what i want to know
above all else-
who wrote the definition
of beauty and why do we obey
its modern stupidity?

perhaps we are all fools,
but goodness, friends-
fuck every opinion
that has brought you down.
you are unique and alive
and wonderful.
just be passionate about
what you love.

fuel your fucking fire.

we build
castles
with our
fears and
sleep
in them like
kings and
queens

when my father was in the hospital,
seconds away from dying from an
overdose, i watched him and wept and
all i wanted was his victory.
for him to show death his guts.
i imagined his spirit saying this
as the earth tried to take his bones

"where lust shines bright than love,
set me free."

if you are not crazy,
i mean absolutely crazy
about what you love,
then i beg you, either find
a way to be insanely crazy
about it or throw it
away.you were not born
with half an ass
human therefore you
have no right to
half-ass the intensity
in which you
love.

i have decided that i will never
be one who is earthly.
what i mean by that
is i refuse to dance with the
mundane.
i do not want a normal job.
i do not want to be the government's
puppet.
i do not want a nice car or nice
clothes or things that require
mountains of money.
i am tired of this corrupt system
that tries to tell everyone how
to live and i am tired of hearing
the words "well, that's just the way
it is."

i will not conform and i
can only ask passionately
and politely that you take my
hand and be free with
me?

"pleasure is the pulse of
the universe."
i think to myself.
"everywhere- sex, drugs, food,
religion, love, ego.
we do not go without it.
it is everywhere.
it is all we have.

the sunset is the universe's
masturbation."

the most brilliant people in life
are the ones who have been
through the most shit.
tragedies, death of loved ones,
countless heartbreaks,
heartbreaks that truly puncture
the soul. they are wise
without knowing it and
that is the most pure,
flawless, perfectly beautiful
kind of wisdom.

i have this friend and his father
and little sister died in a car
accident when he was ten
and sometimes we sit at bars and
drink for the entire night
and god, let me tell you,
there is just something about
his eyes.

if i am honest
i like being alone
because it
allows me to hide
from the insecurity
i felt around
others.
solitude was
an easily obtained
paradise.

I will love
   you
with the dust of
   who i was,
with the skin that
   I am now,
and with the bones
   that will one day
   decorate my
      tomb.

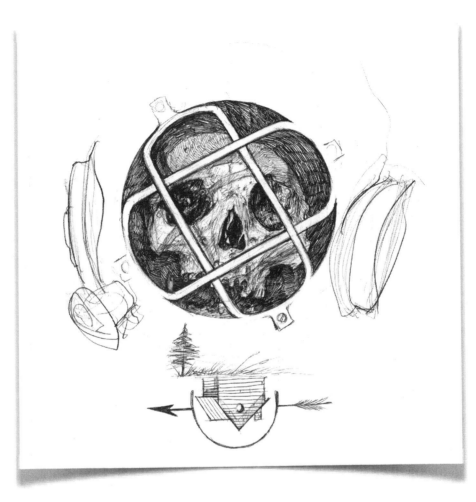

WHEN THE WIND MEETS THE SKULL

i lit a cigarette and wiped
the tears from my eyelashes
and thought to myself that maybe
love is just a rumor that
god stared long ago and the stars
just sit back brightly and laugh
at how silly humans are.

i stood alone in a bar
waiting for a scotch on the rocks
and there was this woman
across the room from me
with this bright and peculiar
outfit on
murmuring something to
herself.
i overheard these drunk
men talking shit about her
"who the hell wears that?
it isn't the sixties anymore."
i wanted to say something
to them but there was
no need.
people will act savagely no matter what,
and i am sure they fight wars
all their own.
besides i think i needed that moment.
it was the first time
i realized how madly in love
with humans i am.
especially the strange ones.
for it is ever so
alluring to be strange.
to do things differently than
others.
to see things in a rare light.
to me, that is such gold
to carry.

this morning i locked
myself in my room and thought
of all the sad, terrible
things in the world.
i told myself "weep, boy, weep."
i had not wept in years.

goddammit, i could not weep.
but i sure as hell wanted to.

the war in my body is
this-
i am always trying
to be a hard person
and a soft person
at the same time.
my flesh doesn't know
which one to be.

everything pulls me.
i am quite the contradiction.

his name was hurley and he spent his life
beneath us. i remember him from high school,
he rolled around in his wheelchair like
he knew something we didn't. he couldn't
speak because of his illness but he always smiled
with his head tilted back when you said his name
as if his ears had been waiting for that sound
since birth. there was something
about him i begged to know. something deeper.
something i knew i could grasp with enough
awareness, enough observation.
he looked happier than the people on the streets,
the people hundreds of floors up in their
comfortable suits, only craving money.
his name was hurley but inside
my bones I named him grace,
and sometimes i dream of him at night
dancing on his feet in the streets
of New York City as everyone
watches with warm tremulous
applause.

i walk outside
and nature kisses me
where it hurts,
her wet lips
electrifying
like a lost lover
returned to
your arms.
i do not believe
in a god.
i believe in the universe.
the stars are my
scripture
and the wind
through my hair
is truth,
i throw my hands
up in worship
and my bones swallow the
moon.

there will always be
a feeling in your
body that is
unexplainable.
one that needs no
reason and it
just is because
it is.

i look at you
and i know love.
i look away
and i know nothing.

she never wanted to have
that kind of romance. by 'that'
i mean the kind where you must be
together every moment of every day.
she never liked the idea
of forfeiting
her loneliness. she felt the yearning to
be held, loved, of course, but with
that yearning also come the terrifying
hunger for separation-
no matter who she loved
or how much she loved them, she
did not want to go days
without feeling somewhat
alone.
and I must say I became quite
obsessed with that.
she could not have been
more beautiful.

the most beautiful people to be around
are the ones with open minds. the one who
will tell you that sorrow is just as
important as bliss and that at any moment,
you can be whoever you want to be and
love whoever and whatever you want to love,
whether it is drinking or the same sex or
pain or a certain religion. i sit at bars and
linger in coffee shops just to find these kind
of people.

without knowing it, they are slowly
changing the world.

sometimes,
the universe is much too
beautiful for my own
good.

sometimes,
you are the
universe.

the word love these days is used
so redundantly.
i am as guilty as any,
but i think words and things become less
meaningful the more we use them.
why do you think I am going to New York City,
my dear?
it isn't because I don't love you.
it is the contrary in fact.
I am going away to miss you-
to spend my nights in new bars and my mornings
in new coffee shops, writing, alone.
to walk the streets with thousands of
strangers all around me and feel small in a
way that sings to a place inside me that
has never heard a single note of music.
to hear fresh laughter and of newly painted
sorrow and stories in bars about terrible
men and women and lovely ones and how
they cannot live with or without each other.
to feel all things in a new city and to be
so exhausted from writing my ass off for
them and you, exhausted in a way that there
will be nothing in this goddamn world
comparable to the way i will feel when you
pick me up from the train station after not
seeing you for months-
 nothing quite as beautiful
and refreshing as the death of missing you
and soon enough the birth
of it again-

for the death only felt so beautiful
because the birth hurt so immensely.

i love
the peace the
sea gives me

as if i am made
from the salt
itself,
staring out
into the swaying
of my true mother.

walking through a city
where the lights are more
than just lights
they are tiny friends
to thousands of
people
i watch these people
they are some kind of
home to me.
suddenly i see
a hole in
the wall restaurant
with one little old lady
sitting by the window
and i can't help
but go in and sit down
in silence
while she eats her meal
and i order mine
two reserved people alone
in one gigantic city
this is what i love
the quiet the strange
the different

the hole in the wall
things
the hole in the wall
humans.

i have never been
one to make plans
i have always thought them
to be a limitation
but the plan
to love you
until i am nothing
has always been
an exception

i find myself sometimes
at night
thinking of you
in colors
as if you are
the world
around me and
nothing else really
matters.

simmer down, lovelies.
lift up your tristful heads.
i promise, someday soon,
we will learn to starve
our aches.
until then,
we must teach our lungs
to breathe patience,
our souls to cling
to hope,
and somehow, someway,
find what makes our
hearts feel a little
less alone.

you are not the woman i wished for.
where did you come from, human?
you are not the bones or the
laughter or the strangeness
i ordered. you do not consist of
the madness i so desperately and
achingly long for.
you are tender and sweet and as
soft and lovely as a bouquet of clouds,
you are more soul than body,
more grace than bones,
more heart than lust.
but, you are not what i wanted.

which analogy or metaphor
or word should i give you
with tears in my eyes to tell you
something that is as simple as the
moon is bright?

you are not what i wanted.
you, are better.

may we carry
a fraction of
each other's eyes
within our own,
for it would be
a shame
to have lived our
entire lives
and know that
through all the world's
weeping and wiping
of lashes,
we only ever soaked ourselves in
our own delicate
tears.

i adored her both
for the way
the air stole the tears
from her eyes
and the way she smiled
slightly because she knew
the universe would never
give them back.

WHILE SENSE IS BEING MADE LIKE LOVE

sometimes
i wish there was
a place in the
furthest
corners of the
earth
where the homophobes
and racists
could be sent off
to
for just enough
time
to make them
realize
that people
are not made to fit
into
the puzzle of their
ill-shaped
egos.

i thought
as the sun
lifted once
more from the
sea
of how truly
heartbreaking
it is that we
all feel
so heavy,
and yet,
somehow,
so damn
empty.

i met a stoner on third street, we laughed
together sweetly and talked about all of
the simple terror in this world.
she told me "i don't understand their
fucking problem. smoking is delightful.
it isn't a way of living. it is a way of
kicking reality in the ass and saying,
'you don't own me,' knowing that too often
it does. their reality is crucifying
because their head is in the ground.
mine is gratifying because my mind is
in the clouds.
do not let them bury you.
stay lifted."

i often feel
unwanted
so i keep quiet
in the background
of those more
precious than
me

in my solitude
i hear secrets about
myself god only
tells to the flowers,
his voice whimpering
from stars to
dust,
from gates of gold
to soil.
he says,
"you are a collection
of all the people
you have ever loved."

i suppose we are all
searching for something
and often we look in the wrong
places
our eyes gazed towards oceans and
universities and normality
while the truth is hidden in the most
unexpected corners of the
earth
like the bright eyes of a beggar on the
streets
or the prostitutes cocky walk
or the doped up deadbeat father with tubes
soon to be shoved down his throat.

remove your judgmental eyes
from the only body
you will ever have and replace them
with new ones and understand
that being human and human alone
is the only reason we will ever need to
love
and understand it so intensely
that as you
fall asleep at night you close
your watery eyes and
whisper to yourself,

"i am human. they are human.
we are human."

today i received a postcard
i sent to myself last week
from another city when i
was nearly too drunk to
stand, it read, "find a way to
fall in love with life sober.
these damn morning headaches
are killing me."

i romanticize
all things.
every goddamn thing.
every thing is not pretty.
every thing is not blooming.
i have to stop making roses
out of guns.
the things that destroy
us
are not always magic things.
ever since i became
old enough
to jerk my own chain
and spill my
own guts,
i have been infatuated
with human tragedy.

cheers to the odd ones
like me.

"i just love too much,"
she tells me,
glass in hand,
mascara ruined.
"be proud of that,"
i say.
"wear that blessing in your
chest like a second heart.
not everyone has that ability.
as ludicrous as this sounds
darling, some people are
just too tired for love."

"do you feel that?"
she asked as we watched
the stars and moon illuminate
the sea before us,
"tell me you feel it?
that longing to not just exist,
but to live and to live
beautifully?
i, with a smile filled with so
much truth it could move
the clouds, replied
"of course i feel it,
the heart in you is the
heart in me.

violence-
a reply to hate
and other horrors.

needed voices-
silenced.

insane voices-
mimicked and
pursued.

judgement-
repeated
and repeated

even by the ones
who preach
against it.

to put it simply as possible,
lovelies,

i am tired of all the bullshit.
even my own.

maybe god is
a pilot
that knows
the plane will crash
before we ever begin
to lift off.
the key as a human
and passenger
is to learn how
to smile like hell
on the way down.

this homeless lady on
third and broadway
she is the solution
the cure for a world gone blind
she sits there with a bottle of
evan williams every night
holding a sign that says, "will love for food."

no one knows what it truly mean
some think it is bullshit
some think it is hopeless
some think it is beautiful

but if you take the time to
talk to her
to reek of her torture
in your own skin
then you would know
she is mother mary
in invisible high heels
drinking the finest scotch
loving the lowest of people
in the worst conditions
on their worst days

as strange as this seems
to say
i think i want whatever
it is she has.

there is a man doing acid next to me.
he says he takes it to meet his
dead best friend in the clouds and
i do not stop him.
why should i? float away sweet human...

we all have our own paradises.
mine is in the arms of whiskey and the woman
i love.
she holds me like i am made of ocean
and i reply to her with ferocious tides.

fuck, that sensual moment is ruined.
the man on acid just whispered to me,
"holy shit. are you justin bieber?"

i tremble naked against you-

your soft kisses are blinks from
the eyes of the world.
my skin is made new again and again
and again.
sometimes i think it is silly to
define what people feel for each other.
to label it.
what is love?
they ask the question but some are
too afraid to swallow the answer.
what if it doesn't need an answer?
maybe love is not just one thing. maybe it
is all things-
the hundreds of glances i give
you each day, breathing you into
my lungs in many ways.

i say if love is anything,
it is everything.

l will never
be a morning person,
for the moon and i,
are much too in
love.

THERE IS NO END, ONLY BEGINNINGS

i loved
the way
she touched me.
what more can
i say?
her hands were
made from the things
we all have trouble
believing.

you have always told me
there are no words
you have been able
to find
that make sense of what
is inside you.
but why should you ever
become weary with
that, my love?
for words are just tiny winds
with sounds of different
arrangements, and even if you
are never able to find the
right ones,
by god if they never come,
know this-
you have always made sense
to me.
even when you are nothing
but shattered pieces.

you have to defeat reality
with that
imagination of yours.
i say "of yours"
because everyone is capable
 of having one.
we have to create our own
worlds and people and cities
that make this life more
bearable when it comes detrimental.
that is what writing stories and reading them
is all about. we sail on the wings of
either our own words or others.

all that i
ask
is that when
i die
bury me
in fractions of
ash
in all of
the cities
she ever
felt
alone.

when will these
delicate bodies
fully understand
that they are not
merely the artists,
but more so,
the art?

you there, made of
colored rain,
of fallen things
that melt into
earth,
i love you, still,
i have loved you since
the day of our first
greeting.
i remember your hair,
your lips
(sweet like wine
a tasteful lover)
your voice,
your presence
(as powerful as death
but in
different form,
pure,
always ready for
rebirth.)

i remember you
as one universe,
an immaculate whole.

you remind me of something
not human.

i have to look at life as if every single thing
around me is a gift,
or else i have no motive, no passion, no fire
from my bones to the world.
the details are the magic. i must see things,
things so small and so perfect,
things necessary to beauty. i see the
crow's feet beneath a grandmother's eye, the age
and determination for a life of peace and doves
and everything after. i see the bottle of booze
at the alcoholic's feet, the love inside it
somewhere, buried deep, reaching
out like a child's hand for their father's
absent touch. i see fingerprints on coffee shop
windows where infants stretched unknowingly
into freedom, their mothers wondering what it
would be like to be young again, oh to be young
again, to be full again.
i see the cries of happy ones, the smiles of
sad ones, the things in-between the spaces where
no one ever roams.
i must see these things with the eye of my eye,
with the soul of my soul.
i will keep them with me like a pocket
on my flesh, i must never be
without them.

i feel you in there.
you do not hide, you claw your way through
but sometimes i push you back in.
my quivering actions pretend something other
than you are my grandest hallelujah.
i act this way out of fear, insecurity, and
false absolution.
this is my oath to you darling, my light
pulled clean from the darkness, bare and beating
like a fresh human heart.
walk with me into the glamour of this-
i am madly in love with you. outside of love
i exist, with you. we are bigger than it.
when we die they shall birth a word only for us.
our bodies are novels not heard yet, not
understood. our eyes ink our flesh pages.
what we write with our days of love
and terror and joy and sorrow
will be put onto shelves of magic and all
of life will breathe in our story for pleasure.
we will die together and live together in a way
no one has ever imagined-
with the abundance of tears and laughter
and passion and truth and the thought that
the human experience is actually worth
fighting for.

some believe, some hope, some try,
some just know. i am the last of those.

these bodies were married long before they
ever began.

we all at times are
filled with a little death
inside
we can only wish
with the utmost belief
that some crazy person
will love us enough
to keep placing flowers
upon the graves
in our hearts.

love is many things
and sometimes we are
never really sure if it
even exists,
but all i know is if
you were to show me
her soul
in a photograph,
i wouldn't even ask
to see the others.

some days i wake up
and think of all the men
before me and the fools they were
to ever let you slip through their
fingers.
they were such damn fools, you know?
they were the type of people to watch
the rain through their windows and
say "don't you just love the rain?"
i, on the other hand, was the only one
to watch it pour outside, take my shoes off,
and anxiously and bravely,
go dance madly in you.

fall in love with
expressing yourself.
it does not matter how you
do it.
you understand, creature?
dance until
your feet erode into
the earth,
sing until
your lungs cave
in,
be silent
until the world
understands
the absence
of noise
is beautiful.

express whoever
you are
because
what you are
is essential.

everyone claims they want chaos
but no one brings their knives to
the table.
we fall in love with the idea of things
but further down as flesh
is stripped away and bones
are embraced,
i think most of us are frightened
at the reality of it.
we are afraid to love what
makes us uncomfortable.

i have always had a gut feeling for the
crazy things. a mad fascination for
the rubble of the mind and body and
spirit.
this has birth a feeling in me that
draws me away from the world.
i love so many things
yet i am alone.
and i am in love with that.

i dip my toes in the flames and people behind
me are in line,
but i sense a certain wild lie
in their eyes.

my father used to tell
me, "son, you are going to
grow up and be somebody."
it wasn't until he returned
home from rehab only
to show us soon he would
choose drugs over
us that i realized
he had always been
flawed in his thinking.
the whole time he should
have been telling me,
"son, you are somebody."

it's easy to feel beautiful
when you are loved,
when stares call your
name
like a stadium full of
hungry wolves howling
for the sight of blood.
it's easy to feel warm when
your skin is made from
purple rain,
when strangers crave
your name by you
simply passing them
like a sun kiss to the edge
of morning.

somewhere deep down
i am glad the gods didn't make
me beautiful.
it keeps me humble.

sometimes i
would smoke
a cigarette
just to feel
my father's lungs
in me
and even cough
over and over
and pretend it
burned
just because
i missed him
and the
sound of his
living.

i think to
crave what
is nearly impossible
to obtain is
just as human
as waking up
and starting a
pot of coffee.

harmony. it calls my name like no other.

the cosmic optimist in me does not make
its bed in hours of the night when my
soul comes out to play with coyotes
and moonlit pieces of earth flesh.

i am everything. so much of everything
and everyone,
that my lips sing hymns,
my neck relives natural disasters,
my chest snorts cocaine in trippy lines,
my waist loves one woman until its death,
my thighs live in motel rooms and
fuck there too,
my knees recite poetry,
my shins pray to jesus,
my feet cut their wrists and
find their end
in the bottom of
orange bottles.

the more i feel the more i realize
my body is the silent pull
towards all things and feelings.

THE UNIVERSE WROTE FICTION IN US AND NAMED IT FEAR

i remain awake in the
quiet hours of the night
when the moon is bold and
beautiful, for one reason,
one reason only- this life is
hiding something from me.
dammit, i know it is.
and the beautiful thing is i know
it wants me to find it.
all the things i do are an attempt
to discover it.
the whiskey, the literature, stargazing,
romance, music.

it drives me mad but it flames
my passion just as well.

so, here i am, universe,
plush with desire.

reveal yourself you beautiful
mother fucker.

from a hole in the wall bar in NYC

the bartender was a lovely german woman,
newly engaged, happy, but still
left with a scent of
something unknown.
"this is my first time in the city,"
i said, after ordering a double shot
of Jameson.

"oh really? what do you think?"

"i am in love. simply. the air here
has purpose. it's quite nice."

she smiled, slightly,
uncovering the thing unknown,
"yes, well, you know what they say.
you always want what you don't have."

there is a balance to human beings
so difficult to understand
it sits like an owl
in the night
eyes large like moons
staring and staring

as the alcoholic father walks into
a bar
as the widow mother shoots up heroin
as a preacher lies his praying head
 onto his pillow at night
as an innocent child gets beat
as a young boy name Achilles
develops cancer
as the sun rises and sets
in the east and the west

as the world just exists
as it so charmingly does

as all things teach us
why we love and fuck and
hurt and judge-

understanding is the most beautiful word
in the human language.

i look around and i see them. people in love
people falling out of it.
my clumsy mind tries to make sense of it
but it's like a game tossing me again and again.
such fiascos and parades.

i have this dream where Bukowski
and Mary Oliver are at a bar having a drink
and Bukowski says to her in his maddened
tone, "love is a dog from hell."

she smiles a smile of pleasure and replies,
"someone i loved once gave me
a box full of darkness. it took me years
to realize that this too, was a gift."

in this dream they are gods and love is
born in the balance of their
poetry.

from wherever you are i know all good
things beat within us. i cannot just accept
this world the way it is my dears-
bloody and lacking love in the hours
when love is needed most. let us rise like
fog in the morning, fill our canyons and
valleys with bulletproof hope. we can be
and do what very few choose to. we can
fuck or make love and believe and take drugs
or none of them at all, it doesn't really matter,
all that matters is that love is the string
that holds everything together.
we can be the ones who don't give a damn
about race and appearance and money and
sexuality.
bring the beggars to us, bring the prostitutes,
bring the rich men, bring the addicts.
we will not destroy any of your humans mother
universe, even if we are destroyed by
loving them.

this is a call for the ones just as sick
as me, ever since i was a young boy,
i always had this relentless belief in
humanity.

some people
buckle
so tightly
to their own
ideas and ways
of living
that they refuse
to unbuckle
and accept
someone else's

watch out for
their horns

they will try
to piss on
your dreams

but you have the
ultimate gift-
you are not like
them

i have learned
there are
very few things
smoking herbs
and being drunk
won't tell you.
if you want
to see an honest
man,
pour him a drink.
if you want to
feel the soul
of a
man,
pass him the
herbs.

there are some pretty people
on this earth, my goodness.
the sad part is it takes most
people a lifetime to realize
what pretty is and
how to see it.
deathbeds are revelations
of our aesthetic existence.
one day it will be much too late
and the
burden of beauty unseen
will hit you like a comet to the
chest,

all i ask of you is
to love what is difficult to love
and find what is difficult to see.

loving her opposed to loving
all the women before her was the
difference in being drunk and being sober.
with her everything around me screamed
a declaration of life.
all the beauty exploded and
what was not beautiful
before began to catch fire.

women like her slay
anything ordinary.

you do not forget them.
they become every place
you go.

if i could
ask
the universe
one plausible
question,
it would be is
she made with a
different energy
than the others?

i am yours.
i am yours as the stars
   belong to the sky
and i am yours as
   the rivers belong
   to the sea.
i am yours as your tears
   belong to your eyes
   and i am yours
   as your lungs belong
   to the pattern in which
   you breathe.

you want me to be completely honest?
i used to be terrified
of love. to slow dance with bliss
and the prevailing chance of
 complete misery.
knowing that, it will either
save me or it will cripple me.
for if there is one thing beautiful
in this crumbling world, it is love.
the curling of souls.
but god, if there is one thing
horrific in it, too,
then it is most surely loving
something with your entirety,
only to have it all vanish
away within the hint
of a second.

MY BIRTH ATLAS

never
ever
go by the book.
they will want you to
but you mustn't.
if the lust is too strong,
tear one page
from a hundred books
and make your
own way.
there is no formula
for life,
no equation
on how to be a
human being.

find your freedom
and breathe there.
drink there.
love there.

i think sometimes i am afraid to say words
out of fear for being like the world.
i don't want to say what others have said
before me.
i want to decorate your ears and eyes
with words that belong only to you.
words that could paint your essence and
yours alone.
you are a magical one, you know?
you are filled with such harmony and every
thing you pass clings to your body,
electric one.
i love you in oceans and galaxies
and the air in-between.
with you there are no questions or answers or
right or wrongs there is only
love and words and silence and the explosion
they all create together
when you breathe is on my chest,
your kisses on my neck,
all that is you into all that is me.

what i admire most
about her
is that she
knows how to
fuck reality
and
make love to
fantasy,
not something
many other humans
know how to
do.

imagination,
is her drink.

i discovered you
in the dark,
when my silly mind could
not interpret things like you.
you taught me everything,
but most of all
you taught me that
every single body
deserves its right to beauty.
big, small, tall, beaten-

we are all different forms
of brilliance.

they ask me how it feels to be in love
to be embedded into another human's skin
but i can no longer tell them
how because my words are tired of themselves.
they are tired of always falling short like a
sinner at the bloodied feet of god
or a druggy with pleading cardboard boxes
as hands.
how does it feel to be in love
i ask myself and only to myself i answer
"why it is wild. it is like swallowing the most beautiful
flowers your mother used to pick for you
when you were a child
only after a few years
those flowers grow thorns and those
thorns tear your insides to shreds
until all you are left with
is a puzzle of yourself
a puzzle so perplexing
it is as if some of the pieces are lost
and will never be returned to you
again.
it is baffling and aching and so much of
too much at times but i swear to fucking christ
i would rather be a puzzle in
a world of her
than a whole in a world
of anyone else.

that is what love is."

sometimes i wonder
what more is there,
insisting within
myself that i
should forget
trying to be
everything to
someone or
something to
everyone
and just remember
perhaps the two
most important
string of letters
ever married
together-

be.

just be.

above all, i just want you to know
how significant you are in case no
other human in this cruel world
tells you so. you do not have to be
a symphony or a masterpiece to
do good in this world.
there is so much love to give and
receive if only you allow your
heart to be open. stretch it out
as wide as the horizon. fill your
soul with all the world's beauty as
the tragic things in your eyes
crash down around you like ash.

let nothing stop you. not one damn thing.

so, i guess all that is left,
that which was left in the beginning,
is to love every single thing that
surrounds you as if death was soon
to come for us all.

it is the way she carries herself.
men beg at the crown of her feet for the
chance to be loved
but she sends them away falling
like dominoes into their own state
of oblivion.
no one will ever know what it is like
to completely have her.
she is made of mystical oceans that
do not crave the kiss of human toes.

i once gave her a flower and it formed
into a whisper.

it said "she is all things men want
to love, but could never handle."

i closed
my eyes
gently
and fell
for the way
i remembered
you-
body, soul,
and all.

i am sorry. completely and terribly. i am sorry
for all the times and all the days and all the
moments i did not tell you how much you are loved.
i am sorry that you ache and that you bleed
and that you crumble so much so that sometimes,
it feels as if you are going to disintegrate into
a million, hopeless pieces. i am sorry that it hurts that much
more when i have forgotten, sadly forgotten, to tell you how
much
i was and am now, mad for even your pieces and i am sorry
if you never felt me when i laid awake through the night
watching you sleep trying to think of a way to thread
you back into something whole, only because i
knew you wanted to feel completed.

i am sorry for the tide that blossoms in your eyes
when you want nothing more than a calm, blue sea.
i am sorry for all the times i cannot give that to
you and i am not sorry for the times you cannot give
it to me. it does not even matter my love,
because you are all and you are everything.
you are the grace, you are the splendor.
you are the heaven, when i am the hell.

you are all, all is you.

i, will marry your pieces.

father-

i abide in a place of numbness,
father you son of a bitch why did i have to
get half of you. sometimes i wish
i was all mother- gentleness kindness
and passion glistening from me. then maybe
these hands would look more like scriptures
than natural disasters. let's face it,
your vices were fire and our family
was forest. i just wish i wasn't the only
son to get third degree burns.
the frightening part of all of this
is i romanticize everything you do.
especially the alcoholism and the
overdoses and the rehab. i don't want to,
but i do. when i see you i just want to
weep because all of this is so
hauntingly beautiful.
do you feel me father as i feel you?

from that hospital bed you looked like an angel.

                                        mother-

                          i abide in a place of serenity,
              mother your warmness is the sun of my soul.
                   you are the reason for the late nights
                crying myself to sleep thinking of homeless
         men and widows and young children with cancer.
                 you are the reason i cannot conjure up enough
                     anger to tell an asshole to fuck off,
                   the reason i get drunk and lie down
             with my dogs as if they were the only thing
            good in this maddened world. you are the color
       yellow and lavender and orange. you are the water
              in my eyes and the placement of my bones.
                   you are all the good in me,

         and it pulls and pulls and pulls.

the truth is when i observed them,
nothing in my life had ever meant more.
they tore off their glowing garments and
presented themselves naked.
they were an open bottle for the world to drink
from.
who you ask with eager ears?
i will tell you, but you must promise me
that you will look for them and appreciate
them, too.
i speak of humans who show no shame or care
for what others think of them-

the quiet girl in a crowd of fools,
the punk rock kid in catholic school,
the gay boy at the feet of jesus,
the shunned the shunned the shunned.
i see them secretly smiling on the inside,
happy to be different,
their eyes a color unknown.

please, please tell me why
the most interesting people
are the ones who do not
live beneath the light?

"do you believe
in the
death penalty?"
he asked her.

"you mean being
sober?"
she laughed.

the universe and i talk most at night.
she is the god of my soul and i listen to her
as if i have no other option.
she tells me about myself and the disease i was
born with,
"Christopher, your life is going to hurt.
you were born with the piercing desire to become
everyone around you. to relate to them and feel
them. your body is going to feel like it is being
pulled a million different directions and that is
because it is. you are so much of everyone and know
that this is a gift. it hurts like fucking hell,
but it is a gift.

my goodness the universe is glorious.

i stared at her moon for maybe one minute more
and as i got up and walked away
into the dark night
i accepted who i was and told myself that i
would love every single human being until
the word loving becomes understanding and
understanding becomes relating and
relating becomes becoming

until
all i am is a collection
of you and her and him
and us.

maybe people are no longer
beautiful to us because
we construct them with our
thoughts,
walking around the earth
building humans
like we are gods.
everything is not always
as it seems, my darlings.
we live beneath
the lamps of our
judging.

i have spent time in cathedrals, worshiped
in churches, bruised my knees at altars.
i have carried god in my pocket like a little
pill that makes one feel warm, energetic,
joyous. i have gotten drunk with homeless men,
smoked pot with strangers,
kissed the devil on the stomach.
i have searched for meaning and purpose in many ways,
howling at truth with bloody fangs,
but nothing comes close to simply being kind.
just being purely fucking generous.

i know my purpose on this frightened
planet is to make people feel loved,
and when i become too proud and tired
for that, give my bones to the vultures.
i would rather be a corpse than be hateful.

lately the whiskey hasn't tasted very well.
i could not figure it out for the longest until
i was taking a sip straight from the bottle
upon midnight and glanced over and saw my
dogs looking at me with sheer defeat in their
eyes.
i sat there weeping and couldn't stand the
thought of how selfish i was. of course i
drink to make the world more delicate and
wonderful but what about the suffering of those
i love?
i take a sip and they ache. i get drunk
and they take in more loneliness. how much
of myself will i fill with me as my lovers
burn in my disease?

i took another sip from the bottle and
fell asleep.

i woke up with swollen eyes and the awful
memory that i am my own bride.

this world makes me afraid. i see so
many things inside of people i have no
clue what to believe. i have no clue who
anyone is. sometimes i want to trust no
one. "if you want to show me yourself,
write it in blood for me," i think.
are we truly the people we say we are?
i have to ask myself that question so often
because you just don't know these
days. i even ask it to myself sometimes
at night, through a bottle of whiskey
and two blunts, i sigh and say,
"boy, you talk all you want, write words
for thousands to see, but if you are not
doing all you can to nurture that
humanity you speak of, i mean all you
can, you are a fake. a no good. you hear
me?"

for fucks sake, if we are going to be
anything, let it be real.

i am slowly and gently losing
the care and passion and yearning i once had.
i used to wake up every morning
and sip a cup of coffee and gladly
watch the sun pour up
from the horizon.
now, the sun wakes up without me
and my body doesn't really
give a shit and the sad part is i know
there is a shit to give.
the world is so terribly stunning
and it is instilled in me to
appreciate that with the highest
wonder, but if i am honest,
sometimes, my bones are just far
too tired to see it.

Lost in loops of memory
declined an unresolved
invitation of a lifetime.
some people want to see
only two paths. only two
options. their choice is
made long before a signal
with rigorous speed. of
course we'll go this way, i
can feel a divine presence
or of course ill go that
way, I feel nothing.
we spoke in glances. beads of
sweat in morse code
dripping down his cheek.
he felt nothing. and for
that what he felt was what
he revived. a varicose
symphony with recurring
themes. I wouldn't wish it
on my worst enemy.*

the drugs worked but left your soul
overdosed outside of your body and you
watched in coughed up bewilderment.
you were never one to obtain self-love
so you hid from your own-
out of mind out of spirit out of
bones.

know that nothing like this defines
you just as no one defines the sea when
it towers swiftly over lands killing
hundreds of people.

all was born with both magic and terror

but i am here to tell you and tell you
gladly
that hope is a bar
in the clouds
and when you learn to love yourself,
as i know you will,
meet me there an

-d i will buy

you a drink

i want to say something filled with so much truth
it will rattle your world. i want to say things like,
"you are more than enough" and
"they define you by image, but the soul is a
grander thing." i want to say "you will find love
if you haven't already and if you have, love is
forever." i want to tell you what you want to
hear and what is easy to say but honestly, there
is a wolf in me that no longer wants to tell you
these things. he believes them to a certain point
but he has learned to harden up, to remove any
falseness and clothe himself with so much truth
that god is no longer a word and science ceases to
exist. the wolf wants to say, "goddammit just be
you and go get into trouble and be strange and
difficult and loving and consume whatever makes you
feel the most in that moment." he wants to say this
because he knows it is what most people will do
anyway and he also wants to do it himself.
we grin at madness delivered to us in simple forms.
chaos so easy to obtain as if we were born with it
in our mouths. i will not try to change you
because change is inevitable but so too, is
remaining the same. i cannot tell you what kind
of person to be and i never will all i can hope
is that you know and understand how fucking
beautiful this earth is, this universe, and that
you love whoever needs to be loved because
love is felt in thousands of forms and i have this
belief in me that if we all strive to feel it,
no matter what form it is in, we will come to the
flaming realization that we all come from the same dust
and all other thoughts tossed our way in
false bravado are irrelevant.

do you want to know how to seduce the night?
this is not a poem about the stars or the moon
because we all know i have overused those terms and i
believe with the abundance of anything brings
with it a deadly exhaustion we all cannot afford.
if you truly want to fuck the night and i mean
fuck it hard and with purpose so that fucking
becomes making love and making love becomes
forever then i suggest you get off your lazy ass and
create art. create it with your soul and your soul
alone and do not be afraid of what
spills out of it. no matter the absurdness or the
darkness or the sadness just let yourself be free.
we forfeit freedom too often for what others think
of us and what a damn shame that is.
to see thousands of people walking around being
copies of an image the world finds so pleasing.
i see too many eyes that look the same and hear too
many voice that sound alike. i see people afraid and
trembling on the inside not knowing
what true freedom is and not knowing if it will
ever be uncloaked from their gentle skulls.
what happened to the beautiful free chaos of
Cobain, to jim Morrison, to Bukowski, to Buckley,
to mother fucking individuals? tell me,
where did they go?

and somewhere in the distance i hear my mother
softly whisper, "son, most of them died tragic
deaths. that is what happened to them. do not be
what they were." and then i realize how sick
i must be to find pleasure in that. to want to make a
difference one of them made even if it took
alcohol or cocaine or weed or acid to do so.

how sick am i? mother? father?
and how sick is it that i take pleasure in it?
that i just want to be what i feel inside for the
sake of goddamn art.

welcome, my sweet lovelies...
to the blooming of madness.

last night i wrote a letter to my brother
explaining what he must do if i die before him.
the letter read, "my dear brother, at my funeral,
please do not let the preacher get on stage
and speak bullshit to the crowd. do not let him say
what he always says when people pass,
"he was a good man. he is in a better place now
and his spirit will always be with us."
make him say the truth. tell him about my
drunkenness and selfishness and laziness
and how i always had a difficult time loving
the things i loved the most.
tell him about our drug inflicted alcoholic
father and how i spent my days
trying to escape the cloned body he gave me.
how one day i was kneeling at an alter
and the next i was drunk with him
in his tiny cluttered apartment.
do not let them dress me in gold
if that was a color i did not own.
you make sure they know who i was
and how burdensome life was for me most days,
but most of all goddammit you make sure
they know that
i loved the human race beyond anything.
that all i ever did was in the name
of human. let them paint my grave
with the word alone. do not even put
my name on it.

UNDERWATER MOUNTAINS PUBLISHING
WWW.UNDERWATERMOUNTAINS.COM
ELIAS JOSEPH MENNEALY & RYAN CHRISTOPHER LUTFALAH
A PRIVATE COMPANY

CHRISTOPHER MARK POINDEXTER

resides in pensacola, florida with his fiance, Lei and their three dogs.

Made in the USA
San Bernardino, CA
25 March 2015